Original title:
Whispers of Winter Winds

Copyright © 2024 Creative Arts Management OÜ
All rights reserved.

Author: Alexander Thornton
ISBN HARDBACK: 978-9916-94-622-0
ISBN PAPERBACK: 978-9916-94-623-7

Soft Serenade of the Frost

In pajamas thick, we dance and twirl,
Hot cocoa spills with every swirl.
Outside it's cold, but we're quite warm,
With silly socks, we start to charm.

Flakes of snow on the window cling,
Winter's here, let's laugh and sing.
The cat in boots, a sight to see,
Waddling round like it owns the tea.

Crystals in the Quiet Chill

Frosty breath turns to puffs of cheer,
In mittens clumsy, we skate with fear.
Slipping and sliding, we laugh so loud,
Snowmen grinning, we draw a crowd.

Chasing snowflakes, we leap and glide,
Until we tumble, can't help but slide.
Giggling fits, our spirits rise,
As snowballs fly and laughter cries.

An Evening's Frosty Lullaby

The moon shines bright, with a wink and glow,
As we bundle up, ready to go.
Footprints in frost like a clumsy ghost,
A dance in the snow, let's give a toast!

With twinkling lights, the trees do sway,
Hot chocolate spills in a silly way.
Beneath the stars, we make our plans,
To build the best snow-people in fancy pants.

When the Air Grows Mysterious

The chilly breeze makes us sneeze and snort,
Bundled in layers, we hold a court.
With frosty noses and cheeks aglow,
We function best in a snow-skating show.

Mittens mismatched, just how we roll,
Sleds take flight, as we lose control.
Snowflakes fall like confetti bright,
In this wintry party, we dance through the night.

The Stillness of Frosted Mornings

The chill creeps in, a frosty prank,
Hot cocoa spills, I need a tank.
My nose is red, a cherry delight,
Sipping warmth under winter's bite.

Down the street, a snowman moans,
His carrot nose has turned to bones.
With coal for eyes, he starts to weep,
'I'm not a snack!' he sighs in sleep.

Sighs Beneath a Blanketed World

Under blankets, we laugh and snore,
While outside, snowflakes start to roar.
A penguin waddles, slips, and trips,
As snowmen snicker; what a script!

The world is quiet, like a dream,
Ice cream melts; oh what a scene!
Chasing sleds, we tumble down,
Landing softly, upside down.

The Twilight of the Crystal Depths

Twilight drapes the frosty ground,
As icy creatures dance around.
A polar bear with two left feet,
Slips and slides; oh, what a treat!

The stars peek out like cheeky sprites,
Giggles float in wintry nights.
A snowball fight breaks out with glee,
'Take that!' shouts one, covered in snow, whee!

Parables of the Nippy Night

On a nippy night, tales are spun,
Of icy giants, oh what fun!
With mistletoe dangling overhead,
The cat plots mischief, napping instead.

Frosty butts on icy chairs,
Snowflakes fall, like fluffy flares.
We laugh and tease, a joyful band,
In winter's grip, we take a stand.

Frost-Kissed Whispers

Noses red like little beets,
Furry hats and snowy feet.
Sledding down with giggles loud,
Face first in a frosty cloud.

Snowmen sporting carrot noses,
Wobbly hats, and floppy clothes.
Their eyes are buttons, what a sight!
Question is, who gave them a fright?

The Subtle Art of Snow

Crystalline flakes on my tongue,
Laughter flows, we're all so young.
Snowball fights with cheers and shouts,
Dodging hits, oh, what a bout!

Puppies leap, a furry blur,
Chasing tails in winter's stir.
Creating tracks no one can trace,
Artistry in snowy grace.

Twilight's Chilled Caress

Evenings chill with twinkling lights,
Hot cocoa warms our winter nights.
Whipped cream snowflakes in a cup,
Stirring joy, we drink it up.

Icicles hang like frozen streams,
Dreaming in our cocoa dreams.
Slippers shuffle, laughter flows,
Wrapping up like squishy snow.

A Tapestry of Frost and Light

Frosty patterns on windowpanes,
Me and my puppy playing games.
Sneaking cookies from the tray,
Who said that winter's dull, I say!

A snow-filled world, a playful maze,
Falling down in silly ways.
With every slip, a giggle grows,
Under the moon, the fun just flows.

The Velvet Touch of Cold Silence

Fluffy flakes dance, quite the sight,
Snowmen giggle in the pale light.
Sleds zoom past, oh what a race,
Frosty faces, a chilly embrace.

Cocoa spills on my warm new scarf,
Laughter echoes—oh, what a farce!
Jackets zipped tight, we leap and bound,
In this chilly world, joy does abound.

Snowball fights, yet no one is mad,
Each icy plop makes everyone glad.
Brrr, it's cold, but we stand tall,
These frosty days are the best of all.

Serenading the Snowy Silence

Penguins waddle with such delight,
Swirling snowflakes, pure and white.
One more slip, will I take a fall?
Giggles erupt, it's a snowball brawl.

Frosty breath and rosy cheeks,
Chasing friends who play hide and seek.
Hot soup warms us inside out,
As icy laughter starts to sprout.

Icicles dangle from the eaves,
What a sight, oh how it deceives!
Sliding down hills, we praise the chill,
Each icy moment gives us a thrill.

Chill-Kissed Euphony

Ice-skates glide with a clink and clatter,
Thick blankets of snow hide all the chatter.
Hot chocolate mustache, what a sight,
As snowflakes twirl in the soft light.

Furry hats wobble, fashion's faux pas,
Laughter erupts in a chorus—ha ha!
Snowmen's noses, weird as can be,
Carrot mishaps bring us sheer glee.

Trees dressed warmly in fluffy white,
Snowball surprises at every slight,
Chasing our shadows, a winter jest,
Oh, winter's chill, you make us blessed.

The Language of Frosted Dreams

Frost-tipped fingers playing at night,
Giggling softly, what a delight.
With snowflakes dancing, tales unfold,
Each icy story worth more than gold.

Mittens lost in the snowy abyss,
Laughing children shout, 'Don't be amiss!'
Sleds spinning wildly, we cheer aloud,
Rolling on snowdrifts, warm and proud.

For every fall, there's a giggle and cheer,
Adventures in winter deliver great cheer.
Cold hands, warm hearts, it's quite the team,
In this frozen land, we live the dream.

A Dance of Ice and Stars

Snowflakes twirl in frosty delight,
While penguins slide with all their might.
The moon laughs high in the starry mask,
As ice skates rare on a frozen flask.

Polar bears wear scarves that don't suit,
The chilly breeze can't mute their hoot.
A dance-off begins on the frozen lake,
With each slip and fall, the laughter we make.

The Unseen Touch of Chill

The cold trickles in with a sneaky grin,
Making hot cocoa with a mischievous spin.
The snowmen are plotting, oh what a sight,
To steal a warm hug under the moonlight.

Socks vanish in barrels of snowy drifts,
While snowballs fly like mischievous gifts.
The unsuspecting cat takes a tumble down,
With snowflakes laughing, they dance all around.

Lullabies of the Frosty Air

The breeze hums tunes that tickle the trees,
As chilly tunes ride the merry freeze.
With boots that squeak and mittens that clank,
The snowflakes form beats; oh, what a prank!

Frosty fingers play piano on glass,
A symphony of laughter as geese pass.
The owls hoot jokes from their snowy perch,
While the winter sun plays a warm, bright search.

Breath of Crystal Dreams

With noses all pink and cheeks like a pear,
The snowmen sit chattering without a care.
Shovels and sleds have their own little game,
Trading tales where the frost takes aim.

Snowball fights start in the light of the noon,
As squirrels wear hats, looking like cartoon.
The icy breeze jests, as giggles take flight,
In the funniest frolic of winter's bright night.

Chill of the Silent Breeze

A snowman stares with carrot nose,
'This frostbite feels like pinching toes.'
The penguins giggle, they love to swoosh,
As polar bears search for a tasty moose.

Icicles dangle like pointy teeth,
Over hot cocoa, a snowman's wreath.
The chill in the air makes the cheeks go red,
While squirrels in sweaters dance on their head.

Frosted Echoes at Dusk

A snowflake lands right on my hat,
I shout, 'Hey there, don't you look fat!'
The trees are covered in fluffy white,
They whisper secrets under the moonlight.

The frozen pond is a slippery trap,
As kids take turns with a wobbly flap.
They tumble and giggle, then shout with glee,
'This winter wonderland's all about me!'

Secrets Drift with the Snowflakes

The hot chocolate's steaming, so rich and bold,
But the marshmallows float like stories untold.
While snowmen gossip about snowball fights,
They chuckle and snicker beneath the starlights.

The wise old owl gives a snowy hoot,
While rabbits in scarves throw snow like a loot.
Snowflakes dance down like confetti so sweet,
As hot cocoa waits for your frosty feet.

A Hush in the Cold Air

The air is still, like a frozen laugh,
While winter critters take their own path.
Hedgehogs shuffle in their warm little den,
Dreaming of spring and sunshine's zen.

In quiet wonder, the world turns white,
With snowball fights just out of sight.
Yet frost brings chuckles, not icy dread,
As we gather hats and blankets instead.

Tales Carried by the Icy Gales

A snowman danced in the chill,
His buttons fell, what a thrill!
He slipped on ice, went for a spin,
And giggled loudly, 'Let's do it again!'

The frostbite dogs chase their tails,
Snowflakes ride on fluffy gales.
They bark at frost, do silly prances,
While icicles join their winter dances.

Murmurs Beneath a Shroud of White

The penguins sled on a hilltop high,
In baker's hats, they aim for the sky!
They race each other, quacking with glee,
Then tumble together, oh what a spree!

The trees wear coats made of soft cotton,
And under them, squirrels are often forgotten.
They sneak on by with a nut in tow,
While birds chuckle at their clumsy show!

The Breath of Frozen Nights

A wise old owl with a frosty beard,
Quips about snowballs he once steered.
His stories of ice and chilly fright,
Make the critters laugh late at night.

The moon donned a hat, snug and round,
As snowflakes played hide-and-seek on the ground.
Each twinkle bright, a wink in the dark,
While squirrels plotted to steal a park!

Shadows Beneath Bare Branches

Under branches bare, shadows play,
Where rabbits in coats hop about and sway.
They trip on snow and chase their dreams,
With giggles that echo like bubbling streams.

The chilly breeze tells jokes in a huff,
While frosty tips joke, 'Is this enough?'
Snowflakes twirl in hilarious flight,
Laughing at winter, what a hilarious sight!

Melodies in the Crystal Clarity

A snowflake twirled, it took a dive,
It lost its way but felt so alive.
With giggles of frost and a silly skit,
The chilly air gave a frosty fit.

In boots too big, we waddle around,
With lopsided hats, we fall on the ground.
Laughter echoes through frozen trees,
Chasing snowballs with shivering knees.

We build a snowman with a crooked grin,
He's got a carrot nose and a cheeky spin.
Then he toppled over with a loud 'thud',
Covered in giggles, all covered in mud.

As icy tunes play from a silver flute,
We dance like penguins in our crazy suit.
With every step, a snowdrift sighs,
Bringing joy to our wintery skies.

Faery Dust on the Icy Path

Tiptoeing lightly on paths of glaze,
We shuffle and slide in a slippy daze.
A sprinkle of magic in the frosty air,
We laugh at each stumble, what a wild affair!

Frosty noses and cheeks so bright,
Chasing each other in pure delight.
A tumblehere, a roll over there,
Muffled giggles fill the wintry air.

Little critters in snowy cloaks,
Join our antics, these frosty folks.
With snowballs flying, we try to dodge,
Oh look! I caught one, and now I'm a smudge!

With faery dust dancing upon our hats,
We make merry with the sleek little rats.
Under the moon, we toss and play,
In our silly way on this snowy ballet.

Secrets Beneath a Silver Veil

A chilly veil masks the world anew,
Unveiling wonders, each frosty hue.
Under the surface, snowflakes prance,
They giggle and twirl as they get their chance.

In secret meetings with the snowmen round,
They plot and scheme on the frozen ground.
With carrot debates on who's the best,
They chuckle and roll, no time for rest.

Frost-laden secrets, all laugh and joke,
While pine trees shiver, and old leaves poke.
The icy branches sway and tease,
In a comedy skit where no one can freeze.

As night falls softly, the moon will shine,
On the secrets we keep in dance and dine.
With a belly full of laughter, off we trot,
Into the winter night, we forget the plot.

Ghostly Dances in the Winter Air

A ghostly figure shapes in the snow,
With a top hat and tails, oh what a show!
It shimmies and shakes in a frosty waltz,
We join in the fun, ignoring the faults.

Through swirling flakes, our laughter flies,
As the chilly breeze brings merry surprise.
Each step a flurry, feet tangled tight,
We dance like madcaps in the pale moonlight.

With snowflakes singing, we twirl around,
Ghostly prancers emerge from the ground.
In this frozen theater, we all have glee,
Frostbitten toes and a shivering spree.

So gather the spirits, both silly and bold,
In the glittering night, let the stories unfold.
For in the winter's embrace, we're never alone,
Ghostly dances bringing warmth to the bone.

When the River Breathes Ice

The river dressed in frosty lace,
Dances slow, a chilly grace.
Fish wearing hats of snowy fluff,
Laughing, saying, 'This is tough!'

Penguins sliding with great delight,
On a frozen path so bright.
Ice cubes clink in their own tune,
Who knew winter could make us swoon?

Soft Serenade of the Cold

Snowflakes whispering like a cheeky ghost,
Caroling softly, charming the coast.
Squirrels dressed in winter wear,
Chasing each other, flying through the air.

Frosty windows with silly shapes,
Drawn by kids in playful scrapes.
Hot cocoa that dances, marshmallows fly,
In this icy mischief, we can't deny!

Shadows of the Glistening Pines

The pines are fluffed like cotton candy,
Beneath their boughs, squirrels get dandy.
Snowballs thrown without a care,
Landing squarely in a frosty hair.

A shadow sneezes, oh what a sight!
Turns out, it's just a snowman's fright.
With carrot noses, eyes of coal,
They giggle as they start to roll.

Moonlit Secrets in the Flurries

Under the moon, the world is bright,
Snowflakes waltzing with all their might.
A snowdrift giggles, comes to life,
Challenging mittens to a playful strife.

The night is full of silly sounds,
As the winter moon spins round and round.
With every rustle, a secret shared,
In this frosty fun, no one is scared!

A Dream in the Crystalline Veil

Snowflakes dance like clumsy sprites,
They tumble down, a funny sight.
Icicles hang like bearded jests,
Nature's chill gives us all tests.

Fingers freeze as we try to play,
Building snowmen who just sway.
A snowball's thrown, oh what a laugh,
Slipping down the icy path.

Hot cocoa spills, a magical mess,
Frothy mustaches, I confess.
Laughter echoes 'neath frosty skies,
Winter's charm is full of surprise.

But in this cold, there's warmth to find,
Rugged hugs and friends combined.
With each giggle, spirits lift,
In frosty fun, there's joy to gift.

Nature's Subtle Winter Waltz

The trees wear coats of glistening white,
As squirrels prance, oh what a sight!
Rabbits hop in tangled queues,
With tiny boots and furry shoes.

Breezes blow with tickling grace,
While snowmen grin with frozen face.
A playful dog leaps to and fro,
Chasing after flakes of snow.

On a sled, we whip and zoom,
Careening down from hill to gloom.
But oh dear, a tumble, what a scene!
Upside down in realms of sheen.

Yet laughter rings through the cold air,
We wrap up snug without a care.
In winter's arms, we twirl and spin,
Embracing joy, let the fun begin!

The Flicker of Stars in the Cold

Stars wink down from velvet skies,
As blankets drift with sleepy sighs.
We sip our drinks with frosty jokes,
Sharing laughs 'round the cozy folks.

Outside a cat, with fur all fluffed,
Looks quite ridiculous, yet so tough.
Paw prints mark a clumsy dash,
In snow's embrace, they fall and clash.

The moon laughs down with a bright grin,
While snowflakes dance, the night to win.
A chilly breeze sneaks up our nose,
Causing chuckles and frozen toes.

Underneath a sparkling dome,
Winter's charm feels like a poem.
With every jest, the night feels light,
As stars wink and all feels right.

Comfort in the Frost's Grasp

Frosty windows, a lazy view,
Cats curl up like little puffs of glue.
While outside sounds of snowplows roar,
Inside we giggle, who could ask for more?

Mittens tangled, a fashion faux pas,
Stripes and spots, an awkward aura.
Winter socks that barely match,
Have become quite the silly catch.

Slipping on ice, it's the funniest thing,
As snowmen steal the show and sing.
With carrots stuck in amusing ways,
Their lopsided grins brighten our days.

But nestled warm with laughter's cheer,
In winter's chill, we hold each dear.
As frosty days stretch out long and wide,
In cozy fun, we all abide.

The Language of Drifting Flakes

Snowflakes fall like tiny clowns,
Dancing swiftly, swirling 'round.
They giggle when they hit the ground,
A frosty giggle, soft and profound.

They chat about the cold, it seems,
With frozen hands and frozen dreams.
While snuggled up in winter coats,
They banter like the jolly goats.

A Frosted Path of Memory

A snowman wore a carrot nose,
He said, "Can't find my frozen toes!"
With laughter echoing in the chill,
He tripped and landed with a thrill.

Each footprint tells a funny tale,
Of slips and trips upon the trail.
The dogs are sliding, what a show!
They sail past me like pros on snow!

Heartbeats in the Winter's Embrace

In hats and gloves, we jostle near,
Where snowballs fly, that's how we cheer.
Each throw ignites a burst of glee,
And laughter's warmth is plain to see.

Snowmen grinning, full of cheer,
Say, "Stay awhile, bring the beer!"
With cocoa sipped and marshmallows tossed,
We sip and giggle, never lost.

The Hushed Charms of a Frozen Landscape

The trees are dressed in icy lace,
They crack a joke—oh, what a face!
Branches creak like old men sigh,
While creatures hide with wary eye.

A fox prances, tail in flight,
He's got a plan, he's feeling bright.
Winter nights bring stars so bold,
Each twinkle tells a tale retold.

Whispers of Faeries in the Snow

Tiny beings dance about,
In the cold with joyful shout.
Snowflakes twirl like ballerinas,
Making snowmen with large pink hats.

Sneaky elves throw snowball cheer,
Squealing laughter fills the ear.
While frost nips at noses round,
They'll melt away without a sound.

Giggling as the snow men fall,
Why do they always start a brawl?
With each flake, a story told,
Hilarious tales, forever bold.

Lanterns Linger in the Twilight Chill

Twinkling lights hang from the trees,
Flickering softly in the breeze.
They giggle and play peek-a-boo,
Saying hi to folks who pass through.

Beneath the glow, the shadows dance,
Every flicker a merry chance.
A squirrel in a hat, oh what a sight,
Chasing dreams into the night.

The cold air bites, but spirits soar,
With silly jokes that everyone wore.
Laughter blends with the icy air,
Magic's fun, so join the flair.

The Frost's Gentle Story

The cold tells tales of playful days,
Where snowmen wear the funniest brays.
In frosted fields, they giggle and glide,
Sledding down hills with uncontrollable pride.

Laughter bubbles from frozen streams,
While icicles sway like vine-filled dreams.
A penguin in boots slips and slides,
Chasing after the fox that hides.

With tales of warmth under icy stars,
And hot cocoa hiding from snowy cars.
The frost has a playful twist you see,
A chilly friend who won't let you be.

Choreography of Fluttering Leaves

Leaves tumble down in spinning show,
The trees shake hands, a comical flow.
Chattering softly, they tease and roll,
In the crisp air, they all find their goal.

They gather round in a leafy heap,
Holding secrets that make the world leap.
Squirrels giggle from branches high,
While a bear in leaf-pants waves goodbye.

With a rustle, they break out to play,
A frosty game on this chilly day.
As winter's chill wraps the earth tight,
The laughter of leaves shines oh so bright.

Chords of the Frigid Realm

The snowflakes dance to silly tunes,
While frosty critters play marooned.
A penguin sings a snowman's song,
   As icicles tap, all season long.

The ice cream truck froze in its tracks,
Two squirrels laugh at their silly acts.
They slide down hills, a slippery race,
While snowmen giggle in frozen place.

Abominable cries, "Watch out for that tree!"
But everyone knows that it's just me!
Winter's jests fill the air with cheer,
As snowflakes tumble, year after year.

Icicles dangle like frozen bling,
While frosty air makes the warm hearts sing.
Oh, the joy of this chill-filled spree,
In the chords of the frigid, wild and free!

Hushed Pines Beneath the Weight

The pines wear hats of fluffy white,
And giggle softly, what a sight!
They bend and sway in a frosty breeze,
Exchanging secrets with frozen trees.

A chipmunk, clad in snowflake gear,
Takes a leap—then tumbles, oh dear!
His pals erupt in snowy glee,
As snowballs fly from each frosty tree.

"Just keep it down!" the owls do hoot,
While rabbits munch on frozen fruit.
The pines sip cider, warm yet bold,
Swapping tales as winter unfolds.

Beneath their weight, they laugh and sway,
With skirts of white, they dance and play.
For in this cool, amusing realm,
The gales of jest are at the helm!

Timelessness of Snow's Embrace

As flakes descend, the world looks new,
Covered in powder, a frosty hue.
Time stands still, or maybe just slow,
When sleds are racing in a row.

Snowmen argue about their hats,
With carrot noses and chomping chats.
"Mine's better!" shouts with a frosty cheer,
While children giggle, full of cheer.

A snow angel flaps, with grace it seems,
And suddenly wakes from frigid dreams.
"Can we take a break from winter's chill?"
They laugh and tumble, the slopes to thrill.

With frozen fingers and layers of clothes,
They sprinkle snowflakes on their toes.
For in this embrace, time loses its way,
As the fun of snow brightens the day!

Glimmers of Light on Frosted Branches

The sun peeks through on chilly morn,
Bright light dances, with laughter born.
On branches laden with glistening ice,
A raccoon spies, thinking, "Oh, how nice!"

Icicles drip like icy jewels,
While rabbits hop, all giddy fools.
"Let's build a fort," they cheer and shout,
But end up tumbling all about.

A chorus of breezes tickles the trees,
Enticing giggles on swirling knees.
Light sparkles shine, like confetti thrown,
As winter pranks keep the chill well-known.

With every shimmer and frosty delight,
The world twinkles under pure daylight.
Oh, how we laugh as we dance and play—
In this sparkling realm, we joyfully stay!

Notes from the Abyss of Winter

Snowflakes dance, a frosty waltz,
Hats blown off, it seems like fault.
Penguins on parade, strut with flair,
While snowmen plot, their frosty hair.

Icicles hang like teeth of doom,
Hot cocoa spills in winter's gloom.
Dogs in sweaters, prancing at light,
Tails wagging hard, what a silly sight!

Funny squirrels stash food with glee,
While they giggle at a snowbound bee.
Chilly gales, a comical push,
As mittens fly in a winter hush.

But amidst the fun and frozen cheer,
Laughter echoes as spring draws near.
A snowball fight, oh what a win,
In the abyss, let the games begin!

The Sighs of a Snowy Landscape

Snowy fields, a blanket so white,
But fellas in boots? What a sight!
Tripping and slipping, they flail and spin,
While the cold wind laughs, let the fun begin!

Crisp frosty air, burps of surprise,
Chickadees chuckle, what a disguise!
Outdoorsy folks, they scream and shout,
As sleds race by, a winter rout.

Snowball missiles fly with a thud,
Landing on faces, oh what a dud!
But laughter erupts, they brush off the fate,
In this snowy dream, they celebrate.

Hats chase each other, it's a mad dash,
While the snowmen just grin, oh what a clash!
In this silly land, joy reigns supreme,
Every cold moment's a laugh-filled dream!

Veils of Frosty Silence

Under layers of frost, silence sleeps,
But out in the yard, a funny dog leaps.
His tail's a propeller, round and round,
Pawing at snow, without a sound.

The world feels quiet, a comedic scene,
As cats in snow drift, "What does this mean?"
They tumble and roll, fur all askew,
While snowflakes fall, cold but so true.

Noses freeze, cheeks are pink,
And hot soup spills quicker than you think.
Scarves fly off from a windy blast,
As giggles echo, this winter's a blast!

So wrapped in warmth, we bundle tight,
As snow pants rustle, what a sight!
These frosty days dance in delight,
With chuckles and joy, oh what a night!

Cascades of Winter's Breath

Sliding on ice, oh what a thrill,
As laughter erupts from a steep hill.
Hot chili in bowls, with snowflakes afloat,
While snowmen plan their own little boat.

Fingers in mittens, they struggle to wave,
With cocoa in hand, they're all quite brave.
Snowflakes tickle your nose just right,
As jests fill the air in the dim light.

The crunch of the snow, a comedic sound,
As snowboards clip and fall to the ground.
The trees stand tall, dressed up in white,
While friends burst out with all of their might.

But soon spring will come, that's not a jest,
For winter's hilarity, we'll surely miss the best.
So here's to the fun, the laughter and glee,
In these frosty moments, we're wild and free!

Breathless in the Oratory of Cold

In the church of frost, we congregate,
Sipping cocoa from mugs that vibrate.
A snowman in a tie, looking quite dapper,
Tells knock-knock jokes, oh what a clapper!

Each snowflake that falls has a tale to spare,
Of penguins in tuxes, in icy air.
A frosty breeze tickles our noses bright,
As we laugh at the squirrels, preparing for flight.

Hot chocolate spills, who knew it would jump?
And marshmallows dance like a bouncy lump.
We cheer for the snow, a slippery floor,
And slide like penguins, who could ask for more?

With muffled chortles, we bounce through the white,
Pausing to wonder, is that snowman right?
In laughter and warmth, we find our delight,
As the oratory chills blend with giggles of light.

Veils of Frost on the Ancient Bark

The trees are dressed in their shimmery coats,
With frost as their jewelry, oh how it gloats.
Squirrels wear scarves, thinking they're sly,
While they plot a heist for the nuts piled high.

Icicles dangling, like teeth of a grin,
As we watch winter's antics begin to spin.
A bear in a beanie, the fashion faux pas,
Is the star of the show, we all give a pause.

Wandering through woods, our giggles take flight,
As snowmen take selfies, their noses in white.
The chill wraps around us, but warms the heart,
Each laugh a bright spark, a wintry work of art.

So raise a hot cider, toast to our glee,
To veils of frost and the jolly tree.
With each frozen branch, there's a story to tell,
Of laughter and mischief, winter's magic spell.

Wisp of a Dream in the Snow

In dreams made of snow, we dance on the freeze,
With igloos of giggles that sway in the breeze.
A rabbit in boots, with a snowflake crown,
Hops through the winter, never wears a frown.

Drifting along with our scarves in a whirl,
The air is alive with a merry old twirl.
Frosted the windows, our laughter ignites,
As snowflakes like dancers dive into fights.

A penguin winks, oh what a grand trend,
Check your hat, or it will take a bend!
With each chilly gust, our spirits take flow,
In this dreamlike embrace, where we let laughter grow.

A snowball, a target, we all take our aim,
Miss the mark, but who cares? It's all just a game!
Wrapped up in fun, here's to life's frosty glow,
In wisp of a dream, let's savor the show!

Voices Within the Intricate Ice

Echoes of laughter, the chorus of chill,
Where snowflakes are cheeky, mischievous still.
An owl in glasses reads stories of old,
While snowflakes clap hands, and the potpourri's bold.

In ice castles built, we wear crowns of white,
Each breath a dance, shedding sparks of delight.
Whimsical seals guide our playful parade,
While the ice starts to giggle, a frosty charade.

A snowball flies by, we duck and we dive,
Chasing the moments, our spirits alive.
The voices embrace, in a frosty delight,
Proclaiming the joys of this comet-like flight.

When winter arrives, wrapped in nimble grace,
We leap into nonsense, and tumble, and race.
In this intricate frost, where the giggles unite,
The whispers of glee echo deep into night.

The Soft Touch of Nipping Breezes

A frosty poke upon my nose,
The chilly tease, it surely knows.
It giggles past with icy breath,
A dance of frost, a silent sketch.

The trees are swaying, doing tricks,
With branches that like to play quick flicks.
The squirrels bundle, cheeks all fat,
While snowflakes dress the world in chat.

The hat I wear, it flies away,
Chasing a breeze in a wild display.
As I chase it down the street,
The laughter echoes with frosty feet.

A snowman sneezes, what a sight!
His carrot nose takes flight at night.
The frost is fun, it brings such cheer,
Making winter a time full of beer!

Secrets Carried on the Cold

The shivery wind tells jokes anew,
Like an ice-cream cone with a chilly goo.
Hidden secrets of snowflakes fall,
Tickling ears when they start to call.

Penguins waddle in their suits so neat,
While frostbitten toes skip a beat.
A snowball whizzes, oh what a shot!
Laughter erupts as the mound gets hot!

The frozen pond holds a slippery floor,
Where smiles glide right and left once more.
Even the icicles learn to dance,
With jigs and spins in winter's trance.

My nose is red, it's quite the flair,
While hot cocoa fills the frosty air.
Oh, the tales of how winter sings,
Are secret whispers from frozen wings!

Silence Wrapped in a Snowdrift

The world sits still, in a snowy coat,
While penguins plot their next big note.
Under blankets, we giggle and snore,
As fluffy flakes keep knocking the door.

The snowman grins with a button eye,
As children whip snowballs—oh my, oh my!
The chill curls up with a frosty wink,
While we strategize over hot pink drink.

Patting down snow, a fort appears,
With laughter ringing, spreading cheer.
A snowplow zooms, a loud parade,
While mittens twirl in a winter charade.

Under the quiet, snowflakes prance,
Daring us to join their icy dance.
Winter gigs in its own funny way,
With jests that never seem to stay!

Melodies of the Persistent Chill

The cold hums tunes like a merry mouse,
Inside a snow-wrapped, cozy house.
Outside, the frost starts to croon,
Under the light of a silver moon.

Icicles sparkle like toothy grins,
As laughter swirls and the snowman spins.
With every gust, it adds a verse,
To the lively song, oh what a curse!

Skiers zoom while snowflakes fall,
Bouncing off cheekbones, so small, so small.
Each icy embrace is a comedic play,
Making winter's game a grand ballet.

So raise a toast to the chilly cheer,
With cocoa mugs and butterbeer.
For every breath of that nipping breeze,
Brings giggles and dances, just like these!

Veils of Shadows in the Snow

Snowflakes twirl like little thieves,
Stealing warmth from our winter sleeves.
Ski poles dance like ticklish toes,
Chasing flakes that nobody knows.

Penguins slide on frosty hills,
Wishing for their summer thrills.
A snowman laughs with carrot nose,
How silly in this icy pose!

Sledding down with squeals of joy,
Who needs a fancy, bright red toy?
Snowballs fly with fierce intent,
And landing soft, a cold descent!

So let the chilly breezes tease,
We'll jump in snow, and do as we please.
With laughter ringing through the trees,
Winter's jokes bring us to our knees!

Shivers of the Solstice Night

Ice cream sundaes made of snow,
Maple syrup drizzled slow.
Frosty socks can make you dance,
All in the name of winter's chance!

A penguin in a knitted hat,
Tried to take a selfie – splat!
With each click and shuddering chill,
We can't help but let out a thrill.

Snowmen prance in grand parade,
While silly crows serenade.
The moon winks, a cheeky friend,
With frosty jokes that never end!

So raise a toast with hot cocoa,
To snowball fights that steal the show.
With giggles echoing so sprightly,
Let's shiver through the night politely!

Songs of the Hidden Hearth

Crackling fires make shadows prance,
Stealing cookies in a sneaky dance.
A cheeky cat, in warming rays,
Snoozes loudly in warm foué.

Pajamas fuzzy, mismatched too,
Fashion statements made by a few.
With cocoa spills and marshmallow fights,
We spin tales of wintry nights!

Giggles echo in cozy nooks,
As we read our favorite books.
Hot tea hosts a playful race,
Cups in hand, we'll find our place!

So gather 'round the glow so bright,
In silly hats, we'll laugh tonight.
With patches stitched from days gone by,
We'll sing our song beneath the sky!

Echoing Silence in the Dew

Morning frost paints peony pink,
The air is crisp, let's stop to think.
'Tis the time for snowflakes' show,
Donning coats that wiggle and flow.

The robin sings in fluffed up style,
While squirrels prank with cheeky guile.
Chasing tails on misty trails,
Where laughter echoes, never fails.

The chilly breeze can tease a lot,
As frozen ninjas, we outfoxed.
With yawns so big and spirits high,
Let's revel in the snowy sky!

So sip that tea, and shake your feet,
In winter's charm, life is a treat.
For in each giggle, joy's not few,
Together in this frosty dew!

A Journey Through the Chilling Veil

Frosty toes in cozy boots,
Sliding 'round like clumsy brutes,
Sipping cocoa, giggling loud,
We build a snowman, quite proud.

Snowflakes fall like silly hats,
On unsuspecting furry cats,
They leap and bound, so full of glee,
Chasing shadows, wild and free.

Laughter echoes, friends at play,
As icicles threaten the day,
With frozen tongues and rosy cheeks,
We share our jokes in chilly streaks.

When night falls, a chilly glow,
From snowball fights, our joy will flow,
Bundled up, with spirits bright,
Our hearts warmed against the night.

The Clarity of a Winter's Breath

The air is crisp, a frosty bite,
As we dash outside in pure delight,
Sleds in tow, we race the sun,
Spraying snow like melts of fun.

Mittens stuck, a snowball's thrown,
Laughter cracks like ice alone,
Our noses red, our giggles soar,
While slippery paths beg us for more.

With hangouts tucked beneath the trees,
Hot soup warms our frozen knees,
Beneath bright stars, we strain to see,
The tales of winter's jubilee.

With snowy art that decorates,
Kids build castles, ignoring rates,
A frosty fiesta none can miss,
In moments like these, pure bliss.

Unraveling Stories in Snowdrifts

Each step we take leaves a print,
In snowdrifts fresh, where legends glint,
"What if ducks wore top hats?" we shout,
As powder puffs spin all about.

Tales of snowmen with silly sticks,
Dance in our minds with laughable tricks,
Snowball explosions, oh what a sight!
We're wizards of snow, ready to fight.

Frozen eyebrows, laughter spritz,
As sledding brings a thousand hits,
We tumble down with squeals so loud,
In winter's wonder, we feel proud.

At day's end, the stars come out,
We share our dreams and twist and tout,
Under the moon's watchful gaze,
The memory of fun in a snow-filled maze.

The Quiet Magic of a Frozen Morning

Morning light on frosted panes,
Tickles cheeks like playful grains,
We sip our tea, a mix so fine,
Watching snowflakes dance, align.

The world outside, a canvas bold,
Splashes of white, bright tales unfold,
A dog in boots prances with cheer,
Making snowballs disappear!

The steam from mugs, a cozy plume,
While snowflakes flurry and softly zoom,
With chuckles shared from cozy nooks,
We swap our stories like treasured books.

As sunlight fades, the chill sets in,
We harvest laughter, let the games begin,
In this calm, we find delight,
Winter mornings, oh what a sight!

Whispers on the Frozen Lake

The ice is cracking, hear it sigh,
A penguin slides, oh my, oh my!
Snowballs fly in all directions,
Leaving snowmen with odd inflections.

Sleds collide in joyful glee,
Snowflakes dance like they're carefree.
Hot cocoa spills as laughter erupts,
While frosty cheeks and noses compact.

The frozen pond's a child's delight,
Yet skates will twist if not held tight.
A polar bear does a dance so slick,
While kids cheer on, "Go, do that trick!"

Frosty hats fly up, oh look at that!
The wind joins in, such playful chat!
In winter's chill, all players rejoice,
As everyone laughs, they find their voice.

The Ethereal Winter Chorus

The snowmen sing, a silly sound,
With carrot noses, round and round.
Their frosty tunes make children giggle,
While icicles play a jolly wiggle.

Elves in the tree sing high and low,
With twinkling lights that put on a show.
Snowflakes swirl like they're on a spree,
And every flake has a melody.

Jingle bells echo in a fun parade,
As puppy paws leave an artful charade.
Santa's stuck in the chimney tight,
What a sight to see, oh what a fright!

Hot soup spills from a giant pot,
The cook slips on a noodle, oh what a plot!
Winter's song, so full of cheer,
Brings laughter to all, far and near.

Frosted Echoes

A snow-covered roof starts to sag,
Under a blanket, it looks like a rag.
Snowballs thrown, who's keeping score?
With a laugh, they tumble, wanting more.

The frost bites gently on curious noses,
While hedgehogs peek from their winter dozes.
The mailbox is stuffed with cards and cheer,
As blinking lights say, "Winter is here!"

Cruising on skates, they twirl and slide,
While tumbling tots giggle side by side.
With mittens lost, they must improvise,
Using socks for warmth, what a surprise!

The chorus of snowflakes whispers delight,
As grumpy old cats grumble at night.
In this frosted world of funny and cheer,
The season wraps around all that is dear.

Chilling Hues of Twilight

The sun dips low, a case of shivers,
As shadows stretch and quietly quivers.
Squirrels gather nuts with quite the flair,
Dressed in scarves, ready for the snare.

Hot chocolate spills on a dog's warm tail,
While laughter erupts like a winter gale.
Snowflakes land on noses bold,
As kids tell tales of winter's gold.

The crunch of snow with every step,
Brings silly grins, a joy adept.
Birds snuggle close in their frosty nook,
Sketching dreams in their winter book.

The moonlight glows with chilly grace,
While snowflakes dance and embrace.
In twilight hues of blue and white,
The humor flows, oh what a sight!

Lending Solitude to the Silent

In the quiet dusk, I tripped on ice,
My boots had jokes that were not so nice.
I laughed aloud as I hit the ground,
The snowflakes danced, such a cheeky sound.

Squirrels in coats, they plot and scheme,
Hiding acorns like they're lining their dream.
I chase them down, they're quick and spry,
As I slip and slide, I can't help but cry.

Snowmen stand with carrot noses bright,
One winked at me with surprise and delight.
A top hat crooked, he gave me a grin,
As I swayed and spun, just trying to win.

The chill of the air wraps around my nose,
But laughter warms where the silly flows.
With each frosty breath, I blow out a tune,
Frosted giggles under the silver moon.

Patterns in the Ice's Clear Skin

On the pond, a dance of wobbling fate,
I twirl on my skates, but oh how I wait!
For the crackling song to call me a fool,
As I pirouette on this slippery pool.

Geese on the edge, in a huddle they plot,
"Not today, human!" they squawk on the spot.
With a flap and a honk, they create quite a ruck,
I wave with a grin, all soaked in the muck.

Patterns like lace on the chilly white glass,
But I'm the main feature, catastrophe class!
With each wobbly step, there's a jig in the air,
As skaters fall down, I burst out in flair.

So I glide and I slip, a cellulite dance,
The winter's a stage, and I take my chance.
As ice melts away, and laughter persists,
Who knew the cold could be such a twist?

The Glistening Shroud of Dusk

A blanket of snow, so fluffy and light,
Who needs a pillow when this feels so right?
I dive headfirst, making snow angels so grand,
But end up with snowflakes stuck in my hand.

The trees look like they've donned frosted veils,
As I slip on a branch, it gives me two trails.
I tumble and giggle, my cheeks flush with glee,
This soft, snowy world is just perfect for me.

Baking cookies while snowflakes swirl by,
Mixing up flour, and then there's the pie.
But the oven's too hot; I let out a scream,
While the cookies explode—such a culinary dream!

Under the moonlight, all blunders unite,
In this frosty domain, everything feels bright.
With each silly mishap, I find joy anew,
Oh, wintertime giggles, how I cherish you!

Bated Breath of the Snowy Trim

As I stand at the door, with a snooze on my face,
I watch mittens fly by in the frosty race.
With snowballs in hand, my friends make a dash,
But my aim's a bit off, and I stumble with a splash.

The carols ring sweet, as if on a tease,
But my voice sounds like squeaks, mixed with sick bees.
With voices that crack, we form our own band,
A cacophony of laughter, we're the Promised Land.

A snowman's hat flies off in the breeze,
He looks quite surprised, like he's lost all his keys.
With each swing of a scarf, he bows with the best,
But if he could move, he'd win winter's jest.

The frost on my nose gives me quite the charm,
With each step I take, it's a laugh and alarm.
In this season's great play, where silliness thrives,
We bask in the glee of our wintry lives.

Tales of the Silent Breeze

A frosty breeze did sneak and slide,
It tickled noses, brightened eyes.
The snowmen danced, their scarves awry,
While penguins giggled and waved goodbye.

The trees, they shivered, limbs in a spin,
As frosty giggles grew from within.
A squirrel in a hat, quite out of place,
Chased a snowball with a funny face.

Hot cocoa splashed in cheerful clinks,
As children slid on icy kinks.
Their laughter echoed through the frosty air,
While snowflakes play tag without a care.

So here's to fun and chilly cheer,
Where laughter sparkles, loud and clear.
With every gust, a joke unfolds,
In the snowy land, where winter holds.

Secrets in the Snowfall

When snowflakes tumble with soft delight,
They land like whispers in the night.
But listen close, and you'll hear the tales,
Of snowball fights and little fails.

A bunny hopped, slipped once or twice,
Wore a snow hat that wasn't so nice.
The squirrels laughed as he spun around,
Making snow angels on the ground.

In the drifts, a lost mitten lay,
A treasure map for the pups at play.
They dug and dived, tails all a-wag,
Finding only a soggy old rag.

So as the flakes fall, dance and swirl,
Join in the fun, give winter a twirl.
For every secret the snow may keep,
A giggle awaits, a memory to reap.

Echoes Beneath the Icicles

Below the hang of icy spears,
A secret party stirs up cheers.
With snowflakes twirling in dizzying spins,
The critters gather as the fun begins.

A hedgehog serves some prickly brew,
While dancing owls wear silly shoes.
They slide on ice with squeaky delight,
Creating laughter throughout the night.

The icicles jingle like merriest bells,
As everyone tips their frosty gels.
A raccoon winks, steals a snow cone,
And a hare hops in, claiming it's his throne.

In every shimmer of frosted light,
Lies the spark of joy that feels just right.
So come gather round, as fun ignites,
Under the glimmer of the wintry nights.

Murmurs of the Frosted Night

In the hush of night, when all seems still,
A friendly snowman, named Bill,
Caught a snowflake—the mischief stirred,
And soon a snowball was cleverly heard.

The skaters twirled on frozen ponds wide,
With laughter and joy, they could not hide.
When one took a tumble with splashes galore,
A seal on the ice let out a roar!

Frosty feathers from a playful crow,
Who joined in the fun, putting on a show.
Chasing its tail in circular quest,
While snowflakes laughed and performed their best.

So cuddle up close, let the stories spin,
Of snowy adventures that never grow thin.
For when the frost calls, and giggles invite,
The coldest of nights become sheer delight.

Tales Written in Glimmering Snow

There once was a snowman, quite grand,
With a carrot for a nose, he took a stand.
But a squirrel came by, with a cheeky grin,
And swapped it for a nut, oh where to begin!

The snowflakes laughed, danced in the sky,
As the snowman sighed, oh my oh my!
With a twig for a smile, he wore it well,
His frosty fate, a humorous tale to tell.

A penguin appeared, slipped on some ice,
Landed headfirst, oh what a price!
The land was a canvas, all white and bright,
Painted with giggles, a comical sight.

So gather round, hear tales from the frost,
Of quirky creatures and a snowball tossed.
With laughter and joy, let the stories flow,
In lands where the glimmering snowflakes glow.

The Dance of Dimmed Light

The nights grow long, a soft snowy glow,
While shadows don capes, in the moonlight they flow.
A raccoon in tights, oh what a delight,
Dancing around in the stillness of night.

The lanterns flicker, with spirits so spry,
As frosty winds giggle, and time passes by.
A jitterbug chase, on ice slick as glass,
While owls sit above, and chuckle at the class.

The trees wear their blankets, snug as can be,
While snowflakes fall gently, a soft melody.
With charm and with flair, the forest takes flight,
In a quirky ballet, underneath the moonlight.

So heed the soft sound, of their frosty parade,
Where joy finds its rhythm, and laughter won't fade.
With each twirl, a chuckle, a shimmer of fun,
In the dance of dimmed light, we all come undone.

Enigma in the Bitter Air

In the chill of the morn, a mystery brews,
With snowflakes performing in their fanciful shoes.
A cat wearing boots, prances with glee,
Chasing frosty whispers, oh what could it be?

As penguins convene in a huddle so tight,
They debate how to glide, in the cold winter night.
With a slip and a slide, a tumble, oh dear!
The laughter erupts, echoing near and far, here!

The frosted pines shiver, with giggles they sway,
In the bitter air, where antics hold sway.
The grey skies conspire, in a playful affair,
As wanderers wonder, what's brewing up there?

So embrace the absurd, let the laughter ring true,
In a world made of pearls, where the chilly winds blew.
With every new snowfall, a twist in the tale,
A riddle unraveled, in the wintertime hail.

A Solitary Cry Beneath the Canopy

Beneath the tall pines, a lone howl does rise,
From a dog in a scarf, what a sight for sore eyes!
It echoes through branches, a comedic delight,
As squirrels debate if he's just out of sight.

The moon peaks out, with a smirk on his face,
While snowflakes chuckle, jigging in place.
A bear in pajamas, snoozes away,
Dreaming of popsicles, and cozy buffet.

Yet, from the abyss, a peculiar sound,
Of a snowman's sneeze—the loudest around!
The critters all scatter, in a flurry of tails,
While giggles unfold, in the wintery gales.

So let out a chuckle, as the night wraps it tight,
In a world of whimsy, under starry night light.
In laughter and joy, let the seasons unfold,
A story of humor, forever retold.

Embrace of the Silent Season

Snowflakes dance like tiny sprites,
In cozy hats and snuggly tights.
The cold winds tease with icy breath,
While squirrels prepare for a warm death.

Hot cocoa spills, what a delight,
It splatters like some winter fight.
With marshmallows as little bombs,
We laugh as chaos, it calmly calms.

Penguins waddle in funny ways,
Sliding down hills for wild displays.
Chasing each other, they take a spill,
Who knew the ice could give such a thrill?

But in the quiet, laughter rings,
As children play and joy it brings.
In frosty air, we giggle bright,
The silent season, a comical sight.

The Canvas of a Shimmering Sky

Stars are twinkling like mischief done,
While snowflakes skitter, they're having fun.
A canvas painted in soft white hues,
A chilly artist that loves to amuse.

Hats are worn like crowns on heads,
While snowmen stand like goofy spreads.
With carrots for noses, they make a scene,
What funny fellows, so silly and keen.

The moon grins wide like a cheeky chap,
As frost bites gently on a sleepy nap.
Puddles freeze where puddles don't stay,
The night is a jester in its own way.

Under the shimmer, chuckles blend,
As winter tales and mischief send.
Our hearts are warm, though chilled our toes,
In a funny chill where laughter grows.

The Sound of Snowfall Whirling

Frosty air is filled with cheer,
As snowflakes twirl, it's fun, my dear.
They whoosh and swish with playful tone,
While hot soup simmers, oh, how it's grown!

Footsteps crunching on the white ground,
A weekly dance where giggles abound.
Look out, here comes the snowball fight,
With laughter echoing into the night.

Sleds go zipping down the hill,
Like crazy rockets, what a thrill!
But wait—what's this? A little slip,
And down we go, give winter a tip!

The sound is joy wrapped up in snow,
A comedy act—a funny show.
In fluffy coats, we run and slide,
With humor tucked warmly inside.

Crystals in Harmony with the Night

Tiny crystals gleam like stars,
Chasing each other across the cars.
On roofs and lawns, they make a bed,
Whispers of mischief swirl overhead.

Frolicsome thoughts in chilly air,
A snowball clipping through your hair.
Dancing shadows under the trees,
Tripping over boots with careless ease.

Frosty mustaches, oh, what a sight,
As parents chuckle through the night.
With snowflakes crashing on cheeky chins,
Winter's laughter is where joy begins.

In every flake, a joke is spun,
As the night settles, winter's fun.
We share old tales while fires shine bright,
Amidst the crystals, we find delight.